THE LITTLE BOOK

OF KILLER SAT GRAMMAR

TOM CLEMENTS

HIT 'EM UP PUBLISHING
CALIFORNIA 2015

TC TUTORING "Making Students Smarter, One Step at a Time" www.tctutoring.net / tctutoring@comcast.net

TC TUTORING
346 Rheem Blvd, Suite 110-B
Moraga, California, 94556
www.tctutoring.net

First Edition: January 2015

Cover design by Namita Kapoor

Special thanks to Niki, Sumi, Sachi, Suki and, of course, Michi

Printed in the United States of America
ISBN: 978-0-692-38951-5

Context

We shall not cease from exploration
And the end of all our exploring
Will be to arrive where we started
And know the place for the first time
T. S. Eliot

What goes around, comes around
Law of Karma

Free Interactive App

All the grammar rules and exercises presented in this book are also available for free on my digital app for iPhones: A Killer SAT Grammar Game. Read this book, do all the practice problems then download the app, which has videos and interactive questions/answers for further practice.

The app is available on my website. Simply click the iPhones link at the bottom of the home page: www.tctutoring.net

Killer SAT and ACT Essay Books

To dominate the SAT Essay and/or the ACT Essay check out my two award-winning books:

How to Write a Killer SAT Essay
How to Write a Killer ACT Essay

Table of Contents

1—Getting Started

True or false: you have to be a certified whiz kid to ace the SAT grammar test?

False, but you knew that already. You knew that if somebody could just explain a few basic grammar rules in clear and simple language — with practice tests to reinforce the concepts — then, hey, how hard could it be?

Exactly. Not hard at all as long as you follow the 9 rules covered in this book.

As a former college English teacher (grammar and composition) and current SAT tutor, I've boiled down the grammar to just those few rules you need to succeed. These rules are not meant to be academically rigorous.

Rather they are quick and dirty game-based strategies that cover roughly half of the most common grammar questions tested by the College Board.

For further study, I highly recommend Erica Meltzer's book *The Ultimate Guide to SAT Grammar*, an extraordinary compendium of grammar rules and usage.

In any case, hundreds of my SAT students can attest that mastering this short and simple list of user-friendly grammar rules is one of the two surefire ways to ace the Writing section.

The other? Well — straight up — it's to read my book, *How to Write a Killer SAT Essay*. Check out the awesome reviews it's received on Amazon from former students, parents of students, and even college advisors. It's even been translated into Chinese!

Or, for really quick study, check out several of my short grammar appearances on national TV, captured on YouTube and available for free on my YouTube channel: tctutoring —

   http://www.youtube.com/user/tctutoring.com

Finally, download my **free** *Killer SAT Grammar App*, which presents a digital version of these 9 grammar rules:

   http://www.satgrammargame.com

Methodology

A big word for a simple question: how is the material organized? Glad you asked. This book is constructed to peel like an onion. As a teacher, I find repetition is the key to learning. It's not enough for students to see a concept once and remember it thereafter. Students, even the best students, need to circle around the concept a few times, taking its measure and gauging its application.

For this reason, my book starts out by elaborating the key rules in context, goes on to show their application in SAT-style questions, and then circles back with a small chapter students can use as a cheat-sheet for easy access and assimilation. The cheat-sheet chapter peels the onion to its core, presenting all the rules condensed into two pages for quick and easy reference.

As the quote from T. S. Eliot in the front of the book attests:

> We shall not cease from exploration
> And the end of all our exploring
> Will be to arrive where we started
> And know the place for the first time

Once students "know the place", further practice is provided in the final chapters, one of which purposely jumbles up the practice questions presented earlier and another which provides a full-length SAT-style practice test, written specifically to test the 9 main rules.

Hundreds of my students have used these simple grammar rules to not only ace the SAT but also to avoid making the most common grammar goofs in English.

Subordination

One of the most important components to good writing is sentence variety, which I refer to as subordination. Strictly speaking, subordination is a writing rule, not a grammar rule, but since it permeates the discussion of grammar principles in this book, I want to include a short description of its use.

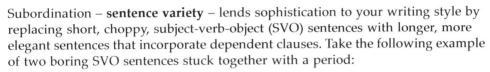

Subordination – **sentence variety** – lends sophistication to your writing style by replacing short, choppy, subject-verb-object (SVO) sentences with longer, more elegant sentences that incorporate dependent clauses. Take the following example of two boring SVO sentences stuck together with a period:

> Rosa Parks refused to give up her seat on the bus. She inspired the Civil Rights movement.

There are three different ways to rearrange and subordinate these choppy sentences to make them more interesting. For example:

1. *After refusing to give up her seat on the bus, Rosa Parks inspired the Civil Rights movement.*
   Notice the long lead-in "After refusing to give up her seat on the bus", which now precedes the subject of the sentence, Rosa Parks. This is a much better use of sentence variety, or subordination.

2. *Rosa Parks, an inspiration to the Civil Rights movement, refused to give up her seat on the back of the bus.*
   In this example, the inserted phrase "an inspiration to the Civil Rights movement" is now sandwiched, to much greater effect, between the main subject and verb of the sentence. Subordination.

3. *Rosa Parks refused to give up her seat on the back of the bus, inspiring the Civil Rights movement.*
   In this example, the tag-along to the main clause "inspiring the Civil Rights movement" is now subordinated at the end of the sentence, creating smoother sentence flow.

That's it. So now, when I mention subordination in the context of my 9 grammar rules, you'll know exactly what I'm talking about. Better yet, check out my book *How to Write a Killer SAT Essay* (available on Amazon) where thousands of students have used this subordination technique to obtain top scores on their SAT essays.

2—Concepts

☰

In American education, particularly at the high school level, grammar is a lost art. The closest most high school students get to any real appreciation of syntax is by studying a foreign language like Spanish, where the subjunctive, for example, is used extensively. Mark Twain famously said "Damn the subjunctive. It brings all our writers to shame." But Twain said a lot of things tongue-in-cheek and where would he have been as one of our great American authors had he not known enough grammar to in fact despise it?

In any case, facetious or not, Twain has had a lot of company over the years. Not just the man on the street — or the typical high school student — but, for mysterious reasons, English teachers as well, most of whom avoid it like the plague. High school kids are pretty much left to their own devices when it comes to parsing parts of speech. As a consequence, most don't know a dipthong from a dangling participle.

All this can be disastrous when it comes to preparing for the Writing portion of the test. If it wasn't enough that kids have to write a two-page essay from scratch for the new SAT, they also have two sections of grammar to contend with, one called "Identifying Sentence Errors", the other called "Improving Sentences". Both sections require knowledge and application of grammar rules.

In the "Improving Sentences" part of the SAT, a sentence is presented along with several variations. Students must determine the best way to express the idea. Most of the variations have a flaw involving some common grammar point. The trick is to be able to separate the wheat from the chaff, grammatically speaking. And this extraction process is exactly what I teach my students to perform in order to ace the grammar section of the SAT. Having taught both grammar and composition in college, I've simplified a large part of the complexity of English grammar down to 9 main points that students find easy to grasp.

SAT Grammar — 9 Main Rules

1. Leaking Oil — Misplaced Modifiers
2. Matching Pairs — Subject Verb Agreement
3. Avoid Alien Beings — Use Active Verbs
4. Shortest Point — Economy of Expression
5. Apples and Oranges — Parallel Structure
6. Mistaken Identity — Comparison Mismatch
7. Who 'Dat — Indefinite Pronouns
8. Me Me Me — Subject Pronouns Never Follow Prepositions
9. Joined at the Hip — Comma Splice

Of course, these aren't the only rules students need to know for the SAT. But in some sense, these rules are *the least* that students should know. In fact, they cover well over half of the grammar concepts tested on the SAT, with Parallel Structure being by far the most common.

But mastering this short list of rules puts students in the driver's seat, minimizing the number of obstacles they'll encounter on the test prep highway and ensuring they themselves don't end up as roadkill!

Each of these rules is presented in context in the following sections.

(1) Leaking Oil — Misplaced Modifiers

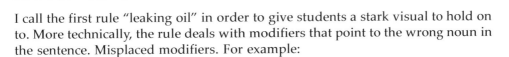

I call the first rule "leaking oil" in order to give students a stark visual to hold on to. More technically, the rule deals with modifiers that point to the wrong noun in the sentence. Misplaced modifiers. For example:

> Leaking oil, the mechanic fixed the car.

Clearly, it's the car, not the mechanic, that has the oil leak. When a sentence has a subordinated lead-in like this, I tell students to make sure that the first noun after the comma points back to the action being described. The sentence should read:

> *Leaking oil, the car was fixed by the mechanic.*

Here's a second example:

> As a boy, my grandma read me bedtime stories.

Is your grandma a boy? Who knows, but probably not. Remember, the first noun after the comma has to point back to the introductory action. The sentence should read:

> *As a boy, I was read bedtime stories by my grandma.*

13

(2) Matching Pairs — Subject Verb Agreement

The second rule has to do with matching singular subjects with singular verbs and plural subjects with plural verbs. The College Board tries to trick students by interposing prepositional phrases between the subject and verb, sort of like stuffing styrofoam peanuts into a Fedex gift box. To get to the gift, you have to first throw out the extraneous packaging. More succinctly: *subjects never follow prepositions*. For example:

> The harmful effects of insulin resistance on the metabolic system is well known.

Notice how the unnecessary prepositional phrases of *insulin resistance* and *on the metabolic system* subvert the true relationship between the subject and verb. The subject (harmful effects) is plural, so the verb (is) must also be plural. The sentence should read:

> *The harmful effects of insulin resistance on the metabolic system are well known.*

Prepositions

Prepositions are place words. Your fourth-grade teacher probably told you to imagine a mouse in a house. The various directions the mouse takes in navigating the house are: over, under, around, through, beside, beyond, above, below, in, on and dozens more.

Still other prepositions point to relationships: of, with, by, for, to

Don't confuse these with other "tiny" words like articles (a, the, an) or conjunctions (and, but, or, for, nor, yet, so).

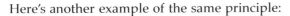

Here's another example of the same principle:

> The production of goods and services in advanced industrial economies are beginning to show signs of decline.

Since the subject is singular (production), the verb must also be singular. The sentence should read:

> *The production of goods and services in advanced industrial economies is beginning to show signs of decline.*

To put this concept into play with SAT-style questions, consider the following examples and choose the **best way** to improve the sentence:

(a) Each of the 5000 spectators are cheering wildly at the game.

(b) The spectators cheering wildly at the game are among the 5000.

(c) At the game, each of the 5000 spectators in attendance are cheering wildly.

(d) Each of the 5000 spectators at the game is cheering wildly.

The answer is (d).

To analyze this correctly, ignore the prepositional phrase in the sentence (of the 5000 spectators) and focus exclusively on the subject, which, in this case, is . . . "Each." Since "each" is singular, the verb must also be singular. This technique for parsing sentences is both extremely powerful and easy, once you get the hang of it. I have my students do practice test after practice test in order for the techniques to sink in.

15

Advanced Analysis

The basic rule of English sentence structure is this: *Subject Verb Object* (SVO). However, more complicated and sophisticated sentences in the SAT grammar section may have secondary subjects wrapped up, like Russian dolls, inside the *Object.* For example:

> Scientists warn that the effect of global warming on ocean currents have not been sufficiently studied.

In this example, "Scientists" is the *Subject,* "warn" is the primary *Verb* and "that the effect of global warning on ocean currents have not been sufficiently studied" is the extended *Object.* The extended Object in this case has a secondary subject/verb pair wrapped inside. To correctly analyze this type of sentence you have to "unwrap" the Object and remove the prepositional phrases that cloud the relationship between the secondary subject/verb pair. For example:

> Scientists warn that the effect have not been sufficiently studied.

After removing the prepositional phrases *of global warming on ocean currents*, it's clear that the secondary subject — more technically, the subject of the relative clause — is **effect** and the secondary verb should be **has**. The sentence should read:

> *Scientists warn that the **effect** of global warming on ocean currents **has** not been sufficiently studied.*

One final note of SAT caution. Sometimes, SAT grammar questions invert the usual Subject Verb Object pattern, placing the Subject *after* the Verb. For example:

> Beyond the Mojave Desert resides the dwindling Apache reservations.

"Beyond" is a preposition and subjects never follow prepositions. Therefore the subject of the sentence is **reservations** and the verb must be plural. The sentence should read:

> *Beyond the Mojave Desert **reside** the dwindling Apache **reservations**.*

(3) Avoid Alien Beings — Use Active Verbs

In the real world, as opposed to the artificial world of the SAT, it's OK to use "being" in sentences that are well constructed. For example: *Being* of sound mind and body, my father lived to the age of eighty. However, on the section of the SAT where students are asked to improve the wording of a sentence, being is *ALMOST ALWAYS* the wrong choice. To drive this point home, take a look at the following sentence:

> The athlete thought being strong was better than being fast.

The verb **being** doesn't supply any necessary information to the sentence. Better to remove it completely and rephrase the sentence like this:

> *The athlete thought strength was better than speed.*

The sentence is now more straightforward and therefore more forceful. "Being" is just sentence fat that should be trimmed before serving.

Note: This rule only applies to the SAT grammar section. In the real world, writers often use "being" in sophisticated and useful ways. I used it myself earlier in this chapter, hopefully to good effect.

Here's another example; check out the selections to see if you can trim the fat:

(a) Jacob has remained in political office for several terms because of being the most popular candidate.

(b) Being the most popular candidate, Jacob has remained in political office for several terms.

(c) Jacob has remained in political office for several terms, being the most popular candidate.

(d) Jacob, the most popular candidate, has remained in political office for several terms.

Which of these sentences is the most straightforward and direct? The correct answer is (d) because it gets its point across simply and directly. On the SAT grammar section, sentences can always be improved by eliminating the word "being".

There is, There are

Another suspect grammar structure on the SAT, similar to "being", involves sentences that start with "There is" or "There are." Both are equally weak since they just unnecessarily stretch out the sentence with wishy-washy, plain-vanilla verbs. For example:

> **There is** a great deal of controversy surrounding the ethics of stem cell research.

Much better is the shorter and simpler sentence:

> *A great deal of controversy **surrounds** the ethics of stem cell research.*

Notice how "surrounds" is a much more active verb than "is."

Cutting away boring verb constructs like "There is", "There are" and "being" results in sentences that are shorter and more direct. And on the SAT, shorter is better.

Note: Back in the day, Gertrude Stein famously quipped about Oakland: "There's no there there." Good thing she didn't have to take the SAT.

(4) Shortest Point — Economy of Expression

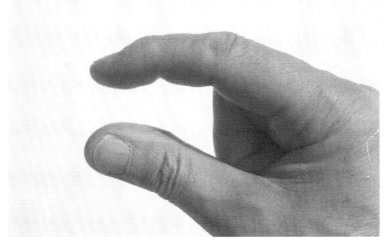

In American English, brevity is the heart and soul of popular expression. Think Ernest Hemingway rather than William Faulkner. Short, cryptic slogans like "Just do it" and "No pain — no gain" are part of the cultural landscape because of the direct way they convey information. This principle holds true for SAT grammar. The most direct form of expression is the best form of expression. Take a look at the following sentences and determine which one says the most with the fewest number of words:

(a) The best way to get an exact answer to the question would be to use a calculator.

(b) Using a calculator would be the best way to get an exact answer to the question.

(c) A calculator would be the best possible way to answer the question exactly.

(d) The best way to get an exact answer is to use a calculator.

Clearly, (d) is the most economical expression and therefore the best choice. As a bonus, this rule can be used in conjunction with other rules to whittle down the possible choices. To demonstrate this, take another look at the examples we used for the Leaking Oil rule:

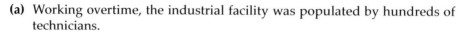

(a) Working overtime, the industrial facility was populated by hundreds of technicians.

(b) The industrial facility, working overtime, had hundreds of busy technicians.

(c) Technicians, busy at the industrial facility, would be working overtime.

(d) The busy technicians at the industrial facility were the ones who worked overtime

(e) Working overtime, busy technicians populated the industrial facility.

Notice that the correct answer (d) is also the answer with the fewest words. As long as a sentence is grammatically correct, the shortest point is the best choice.

There is, however, one important exception to this rule. Parallel structure is the only thing that beats Shortest Point.

(5) Apples and Oranges — Parallel Structure

One of the most important qualities of good grammar — and therefore good writing — is to keep your sentences on track, tightly focused on the message you intend to convey. If you're talking about apples, don't suddenly switch to oranges. Yes, they're both fruit but no, they're not the same. Compare apples to apples and oranges to oranges.

This is important since it turns out that parallel structure is the single most dominant topic covered in SAT grammar. Parallel structure questions are ubiquitous and nuanced, ranging from easy to medium to hard. This section, necessarily longer and developed a little differently than the other Rules, will cover all these bases.

21

≡

(a) Verb forms should be parallel

For example:

> **bad:** Members of the Wyoming Wilderness club like to hunt, swim and fishing.
>
> **better:** *Members of the Wyoming Wilderness club like to hunt, swim and fish.*
>
> **bad:** Most people agree that it's faster to fly than driving a car
>
> **better:** *Most people agree that it's faster to fly than* **to drive***.*

(b) Noun forms should be parallel

For example:

> **bad:** Tupac Shakur was a rapper, actor and he wrote his own poetry.
>
> **better:** *Tupac Shakur was a rapper, actor and poet.*

(c) Conjunctions like not only . . . but also should be parallel

For example:

> **bad:** The judge not only sentenced the prisoner to life he also confiscated his property.
>
> **better:** *The judge not only sentenced the prisoner to life* **but also** *confiscated his property.*

Here are some other common conjunctions, demonstrated in pairs:

so . . . that

> **bad:** The competition was of such enormous difficulty so only the most talented were able to finish.
>
> **better:** *The competition was of such enormous difficulty* **that** *only the most talented were able to finish.*

neither . . . nor

> **bad:** Neither the sports writers at the game or the athletes themselves noticed the hush that came over the stadium.
>
> **better:** *Neither the sports writers at the game* **nor** *the athletes themselves noticed the hush that came over the stadium.*

either . . . or

> **bad:** The captain of the sinking vessel was advised to either lower the lifeboats in order to avoid facing criminal charges.
>
> **better:** *The captain of the sinking vessel was advised to either lower the lifeboats* **or** *face criminal charges.*

as . . . as

> **bad:** In poker, it's often as important to play well than to play lucky.
>
> **better:** *In poker, it's often as important to play well **as** to play lucky.*

(d) Confusion sometimes arises when past tense is inadvertently paired up with present tense

> **bad:** Regardless of where they register or where they lived, voters must perform jury duty.
>
> **better:** *Regardless of where they register or where they **live**, voters must perform jury duty.*

(e) Some of the more difficult parallel structure questions stress finesse and simplicity

> **bad:** Corporate shareholders seem more concerned with short-term profits than they do with long-term gains.
>
> **better:** *Corporate shareholders seem more concerned with short-term profits **than long-term gains**.*

(f) Others violate the shortest point rule and actually make the sentence longer — but tighter

> **bad:** The main reasons criminals give for ending up in jail are that they had difficult childhoods in addition to leaving school at an early age.
>
> **better:** *The main reasons criminals give for ending up in jail are that they had difficult childhoods and **that they** had to leave school at an early age.*

(g) Be careful when enumerating lists to stay parallel

> **bad:** Jane went to the store to buy coffee, tea, in addition to milk.
>
> **better:** *Jane went to the store to buy coffee, tea **and milk**.*
>
> **bad:** Jane went to the store to buy coffee, tea, as well as milk.
>
> **better:** *Jane went to the store to buy coffee, tea **and milk**.*

(h) Finally, some things just go together

Coffee and cream, Romeo and Juliet, death and taxes.

This is true for some noun/preposition and verb/preposition pairs, which (sorry) need to be memorized.

For example: compared with, identical to, different from (not different than!), related to, preoccupation with, capable of, need for, approve of, insist on, interest in, amused by, asserted that.

See the internet for an exhaustive list; search under *verb preposition pairs* and *noun preposition pairs*.

(6) Mistaken Identity — Comparison Mismatch

A special subcategory of parallel structure involves mismatches, where one type of noun is mistakenly compared to another. Take a look at the following examples and see if you can spot the error.

Example 1: The novels of Ernest Hemingway are shorter than William Gaddis.

Example 2: The skyscrapers in New York are bigger than San Francisco.

The first example compares novels to people. The second compares skyscrapers to cities. Both need to be made longer in order to be grammatically correct.

Example 1: *The novels of Ernest Hemingway are shorter than **the novels** of William Gaddis.*

Example 2: *The skyscrapers in New York are bigger than **those in** San Francisco.*

These examples are both longer than their incorrect counterparts but the extra words add precision and clarity.

Lions and Tigers and Bears

Another aspect of mistaken identity involves the difference between comparative and superlative forms. When you are comparing two things, the comparison requires the use of "between" and either "er" or "more." For example:

Between lions and tigers, the lion is the **stronger**.

However, when comparing **three** or more things, use "among" and either "est" or "most". For example:

Among lions and tigers and bears, oh my, the lion is the **strongest**.

(7) Who 'Dat — Indefinite Pronouns

As you can probably surmise by now, the College Board is not your friend. Too many traps, too many trick questions. In many cases, it seems the test is rigged to lure students into making incorrect choices, setting them up to fail. This is nowhere more evident than with the vague and unnecessary pronouns that litter the grammar landscape. Take a look:

Example 1: When Frannie and Zooey went for a winter walk, she forgot to bring her umbrella

Example 2: In New York, they like bagels.

In the first example, **who** forgot her umbrella, Frannie or Zooey?

And the second example, **who**, in New York, likes bagels? Eli Manning, Alvin Ailey dancers, off-broadway actors? Use a picture word, something the reader can see, not a fuzzy indefinite pronoun.

≡

TMI (too many its)

A corollary to this rule is simple: always be suspicious of unnecessary "it" and "it's" used in SAT sentences. (Don't worry about the possessive form "its" since this is usually OK). For example:

> It was so expensive that no one wanted it.

In this example, **what** was so expensive? A Tiffany bracelet? An Andy Warhol painting? Be specific. Jimmy Choo shoes!

Keep this mantra in mind: **It's NOT it.** Define your terms.

Here's another example:

> By the time he finished composing it, his personal life was troubled by increasing deafness.

This sentence has two pronoun flaws: **Who** composed **What**? The sentence should read:

> *By the time **Beethoven** finished composing **his Fifth symphony**, his personal life was troubled by increasing deafness.*

Finally, this rule also applies to adverbs like "then" or "there". To push this idea to the extreme, here are three terrible pronoun-and-adverb deranged SAT sentences:

> I did it.

> I did it then.

> I did it there.

What, when and where?

Golden rule: Never end an SAT sentence with *it, then,* or *there*!

(8) Me Me Me — Pronouns after Prepositions

A fundamental rule that gets shredded in the vernacular but which must be carefully adhered to on the SAT grammar test is that subject pronouns (I, we, they, he, she) NEVER follow prepositions. Instead use me, us, them, him, or her.

How often have you heard people say: for you and I, between you and I, with you and I, about you and I and so on?

On the street you may get away with this faux pas but not on the SAT. The correct expression is: for you and *ME*, between you and *ME*, with you and *ME*, about you and *ME* and so on.

This rule is really a special case — for pronouns — of the rule we saw earlier in Subject Verb Agreement.

Just as **subjects never follow prepositions**, subject pronouns never follow prepositions.

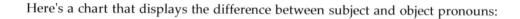

Here's a chart that displays the difference between subject and object pronouns:

Subject Pronouns	Object Pronouns
I	me
we	us
he	him
she	her
they	them
you	you

In general, the rule is this: subject pronouns come before the verb, object pronouns come after the verb and after prepositions.

> **Example 1**: We the people proclaim our independence.

> **Example 2**: The revolutionary council gave **them** the proclamations to distribute.

> **Example 3**: Security guards walked with **us** across the compound.

The exception to the rule involves **than**, which is an adverb, not a preposition, and requires a subject pronoun.

> **Example 1**: Steven Hawking, the famous theoretical physicist, is smarter **than** I.

> **Example 2**: The French drink more red wine than **we**.

Those two sentences sound weird, I agree, but this is a grammar test, not a street fest.

(9) Joined at the Hip — Comma Splice

The last rule is in some sense the easiest; nonetheless students often fail to recognize the ploy, lulled to sleep by the defective punctuation. For example:

> San Francisco is a small city with a large population, this results in a great deal of traffic congestion.

This is really two sentences joined at the hip that need to be surgically separated, using a semicolon or employing different phrasing. More technically, this is referred to as a *comma splice*.

A comma splice refers to two sentences incorrectly connected by a comma. Use a semicolon or make part of one sentence subordinate to the other.

Here are two common ways to correct the problem:

29

(a) Use a semicolon

San Francisco is a small city with a large population; this results in a great deal of traffic congestion.

(b) Subordinate one part of the sentence to the other

San Francisco is a small city with a large population, resulting in a great deal of traffic congestion.

A third way is also possible: using conjunctions like *however, therefore, thus* preceded by a semicolon and followed by a comma. For example:

Napoleon marched into Russia in 1812 expecting a quick and easy victory; however, the cruel Russian winter decimated his troops and weakened French military dominance.

In other words, when a conjunction like "however" is used BETWEEN sentences, be sure to use a semicolon before and a comma after.

Note: This rule holds true only when conjunctions are used to hold two sentences together. A semicolon is not needed, for example, in the following sentence: *The weather, however, was bad.*

Conclusion

Of course, it's not enough to simply present the 9 main grammar rules to students and expect them to immediately put the concepts into play. Practice makes perfect. And not just any kind of practice.

In addition to the practice provided in the following chapters, I have all my students purchase and use tests from the Official SAT Study Guide published by the College Board. To be successful in war, you have to meet the enemy on his own ground. No better place to start than tests prepared by the enemy itself.

After a little practice, my students tell me these rules provide all the ammunition they need to be successful on the SAT front. A little intuition, a little common sense and a large dose of these SAT grammar rules ensure top scores in the Writing section of the SAT.

3—Application

You know the old saying: "Those who can, do; those who can't, teach". Well, in this chapter I'm going to give the lie to that assumption and teach you *to do*.

Having seen all 9 grammar concepts, it's time for analysis and action. We'll circle back through the concepts, include some previous examples to ensure they sink in, demonstrate concise analysis of the 9 grammar rules, and add even more examples to sweeten the total application pot.

Leaking Oil

Read, analyze and correct. The first two questions reinforce examples seen earlier. You can skip them if you think you've got the concept down cold. But better safe than sorry.

1. Leaking oil, the mechanic fixed the car.

   Analysis: What — or in this case, who — is leaking oil? Look at the first noun (mechanic) after the comma and determine what it is pointing back to. Clearly, it's the car, not the mechanic that has the oil leak.

   Action: When you see a sentence that has a subordinated lead-in like this, always make sure that the first noun after the comma points back to the action being described.

   Correction: The sentence should read:

   Leaking oil, the car was fixed by the mechanic.

2. As a boy, my grandma read me bedtime stories.

   Analysis: Is your grandma a boy? Look at the first noun (grandma) after the comma and determine what it is pointing back to. Clearly, your grandma is not a boy!

   Action: When you see a sentence that has a subordinated lead-in like this, always make sure that the first noun after the comma points back to the action being described.

Correction: The sentence should read:

As a boy, I was read bedtime stories by my grandma.

3. Throwing a temper tantrum, the teacher reprimanded the four-year-old.

   Analysis: Who is throwing the tantrum? Look at the first noun (the teacher) after the comma and determine what it is pointing back to. Clearly, the teacher is not throwing a temper tantrum.

   Action: When you see a sentence that has a subordinated lead-in like this, always make sure that the first noun after the comma points back to the action being described.

   Correction: The sentence should read:

   Throwing a temper tantrum, the four-year-old was reprimanded by the teacher.

4. Demolishing everything in its path, the house failed to withstand the hurricane.

   Analysis: What is demolishing everything in its path? Look at the first noun (the house) after the comma and determine what it is pointing back to. Clearly, the house is not demolishing everything in its path.

   Action: When you see a sentence that has a subordinated lead-in like this, always make sure that the first noun after the comma points back to the action being described.

   Correction: The sentence should read:

   Demolishing everything in its path, the hurricane destroyed the house.

5. Sweating profusely, the suspicious device was defused by the bomb squad.

   Analysis: Who is sweating profusely? Look at the first noun (the device) after the comma and determine what it is pointing back to. Clearly, the suspicious device was not sweating profusely.

   Action: When you see a sentence that has a subordinated lead-in like this, always make sure that the first noun after the comma points back to the action being described.

   Correction: The sentence should read:

   Sweating profusely, the bomb squad defused the suspicious device.

6. Working overtime, the industrial facility was populated by the busy technicians.

   Analysis: Who is working overtime? Look at the first noun (the facility) after the comma and determine what it is pointing back to. Clearly, the industrial facility was not working overtime.

Action: When you see a sentence that has a subordinated lead-in like this, always make sure that the first noun after the comma points back to the action being described.

Correction: The sentence should read:

Working overtime, the busy technicians populated the industrial facility.

7. Returning home from the war, a parade was held for the wounded soldiers.

   Analysis: Who is returning home? Look at the first noun (a parade) after the comma and determine what it is pointing back to. Clearly, the parade was not returning home from the war.

   Action: When you see a sentence that has a subordinated lead-in like this, always make sure that the first noun after the comma points back to the action being described.

   Correction: The sentence should read:

   Returning home from the war, the wounded soldiers were given a parade.

8. A victim of mistaken identity, the judge ordered the prisoner released.

   Analysis: Who is the victim of mistaken identity? Look at the first noun (the judge) after the comma and determine what it is pointing back to. Clearly, the judge was not a victim of mistaken identity.

   Action: When you see a sentence that has a subordinated lead-in like this, always make sure that the first noun after the comma points back to the action being described.

   Correction: The sentence should read:

   A victim of mistaken identity, the prisoner was released by the judge.

Matching Pairs

Read, analyze and correct. The first question reinforces an example seen earlier. You can skip it if you think you've got the concept down cold. My advice: just do it!

1. The effects of sugar on insulin resistance is observed in many diabetics.

   Analysis: What is the subject of this sentence? Remember, subjects never follow prepositions like of and on. Eliminate the prepositional phrase *of sugar on insulin resistance.*

   Action: The subject of the sentence is effects. Therefore the verb must be plural. The other nouns in the sentence follow prepositions (of and on) and therefore can't be subjects.

Correction: The sentence should read:

The effects of sugar on insulin resistance are observed in many diabetics.

2. Each of the dogs harnessed in their cages were ready to depart.

   Analysis: What is the subject of this sentence? Remember, subjects never follow prepositions like of and in. Eliminate the prepositional phrase *of the dogs harnessed in their cages*.

   Action: The subject of the sentence is each. Therefore the verb must be singular. The other nouns follow prepositions (of and in) and therefore can't be subjects.

   Correction: The sentence should read:

   Each of the dogs harnessed in their cages was ready to depart.

3. Of all the factors at play in his decision, truth over politics reign supreme.

   Analysis: What is the subject of this sentence? Remember, subjects never follow prepositions like of and in. Eliminate the prepositional phrase *Of all the factors at play in his decision*. Next eliminate the prepositional phrase *over politics*.

   Action: The subject of the sentence is truth. Therefore the verb must be singular. The other nouns follow prepositions ("of" and "in" and "over") and therefore can't be subjects.

   Correction: The sentence should read:

   Of all the factors at play in his decision, truth over politics reigns supreme.

4. The fossil records found in the Gobi desert conclusively demonstrates the theory of evolution.

   Analysis: What is the subject of this sentence? Remember, subjects never follow prepositions like in. Eliminate the prepositional phrase *in the Gobi desert*.

   Action: The subject of the sentence is records. Therefore the verb must be plural. The other noun follows a preposition (in) and therefore can't be the subject.

   Correction: The sentence should read:

   The fossil records found in the Gobi desert conclusively demonstrate the theory of evolution.

5. The first of many issues debated by the House of Representatives are on CNN today.

   Analysis: What is the subject of this sentence? Remember, subjects never follow prepositions like of or by. Eliminate the prepositional phrases *of many issues debated by the House of Representatives*.

Action: The subject of the sentence is first. Therefore the verb must be singular. The other nouns follow prepositions (of and by) and therefore can't be subjects.

Correction: The sentence should read:

The first of many issues debated by the House of Representatives is on CNN today.

6. Shakespeare's characters, personified by Romeo and Juliet, are often referred to as star-crossed lovers.

   Analysis: What is the subject of this sentence? Does the subject agree with the verb?

   Action: The subject of the sentence is characters. Therefore the verb must be plural. The other nouns follow prepositions (by) and therefore can't be subjects.

   Correction: The sentence is correct as written. Gotcha!

7. This is one of the few coffee shops serving food and drinks that stay open late.

   Analysis: What is the subject of this sentence? Does the subject agree with the verb?

   Action: This example is really two sentences, one wrapped inside the other like Russian dolls. Focus on the part that begins: one of the few coffee shops serving food and drinks that stay open late. Ignore the prepositional phrase *of the few coffee shops serving food and drinks* since subjects never follow prepositions. One is singular so the verb should also be singular.

   Correction: The sentence should read:

   This is one of the few coffee shops serving food and drinks that stays open late.

8. Just outside the city is the deserted campgrounds of the army.

   Analysis: What is the subject of this sentence? Does the subject agree with the verb?

   Action: In this sentence the subject actually comes after the verb. Since *Just outside the city* is a prepositional phrase, city can't be the subject (remember: subjects never follow prepositions). The subject is campgrounds. Therefore the verb must be plural.

   Correction: The sentence should read:

   Just outside the city are the deserted campgrounds of the army.

Avoid Alien Beings

Read, analyze and correct. You know the drill by now.

1. The athlete thought being strong was better than being fast.

   Analysis: Avoid alien beings. Think about making the sentence more direct, less wordy.

   Action: Delete *being* from the sentence.

   Correction: The sentence should read:

   The athlete thought strength was better than speed.

2. Being captivated by the dancers, the audience applauded wildly.

   Analysis: Avoid alien beings. Think about making the sentence more direct, less wordy.

   Action: Delete *being* from the sentence.

   Correction: The sentence should read:

   Captivated by the dancers, the audience applauded wildly.

3. The captain of the ship, being asleep at the wheel, failed in his maritime duties.

   Analysis: Avoid alien beings. Think about making the sentence more direct, less wordy.

   Action: Delete *being* from the sentence.

   Correction: The sentence should read:

   Asleep at the wheel, the captain of the ship failed in his maritime duties.

4. The defendant was assumed guilty, being silent.

   Analysis: Avoid alien beings. Think about making the sentence more direct, less wordy.

   Action: Delete *being* from the sentence.

   Correction: The sentence should read:

   The silent defendant was assumed guilty.

5. Rachel has remained in office for several terms, being the most popular candidate.

   Analysis: Avoid alien beings. Think about making the sentence more direct, less wordy.

   Action: Delete *being* from the sentence.

Correction: The sentence should read:

Rachel, the most popular candidate, has remained in office for several terms.

6. Beaten by the gang and being left for dead, the victim nonetheless survived.

   Analysis: Avoid alien beings. Think about making the sentence more direct, less wordy.

   Action: Delete *being* from the sentence.

   Correction: The sentence should read:

   Beaten by the gang and left for dead, the victim nonetheless survived.

7. The patient being better this week than last was finally released from the hospital.

   Analysis: Avoid alien beings. Think about making the sentence more direct, less wordy.

   Action: Delete *being* from the sentence.

   Correction: The sentence should read:

   Better this week than last, the patient was finally released from the hospital.

Shortest Point

Read, analyze and correct.

1. The fastest way to get an exact answer to the question would be to use a calculator.

   Analysis: Think about making the sentence shorter and more direct. Do we really need a conditional verb (would)?

   Action: Make the sentence more direct.

   Correction: The sentence should read:

   Using a calculator is the fastest way to get an exact answer.

2. He left the company and later decided that it was a bad decision.

   Analysis: Think about making the sentence shorter and more direct. Do we really need the unnecessary pronouns — he and it?

   Action: Get rid of the unnecessary pronouns — he and it.

   Correction: The sentence should read:

   Leaving the company was later seen as a bad decision.

3. On the SAT grammar test, shorter is better.

   Analysis: Well, right — shorter is better.

   Action: The sentence is already short and therefore sweet. Leave it as is.

   Correction: No mistake.

4. Receiving a failing grade was when the student dropped out of school.

   Analysis: This sentence is awkwardly phrased. Think about making it more direct.

   Action: Get rid of the awkward phrase — was when.

   Correction: The sentence should read:

   Receiving a failing grade, the student dropped out of school.

5. The busy technicians at the industrial facility were the ones who worked overtime.

   Analysis: This sentence is awkwardly phrased. Think about making it more direct.

   Action: Get rid of the awkward phrase — were the ones.

   Correction: The sentence should read:

   Working overtime, the busy technicians populated the industrial facility.

6. It was important, the coach explained, for his players to understand that it would take hard work and effort to be successful on the football field.

   Analysis: Think about making the sentence shorter and more direct. Do we really need this many its?

   Action: As we'll see later in Rule 6: It's not it!

   Correction: The sentence should read:

   The coach explained that hard work and effort were important for success on the football field.

Apples and Oranges

Read, analyze and correct.

1. Members of the Wyoming Wilderness club like to hunt, swim and fishing.

   Analysis: Verb forms should be parallel.

   Action: Make the sentence parallel by eliminating the "ing" on the last noun.

   Correction: The sentence should read:

   Members of the Wyoming Wilderness club like to hunt, swim and fish.

2. Most people agree that it's faster to fly than driving a car.

   Analysis: Verb forms should be parallel.

   Action: Make the sentence parallel using "to drive" instead of "driving".

   Correction: The sentence should read:

   Most people agree that it's faster to fly than to drive.

3. Tupac Shakur was a rapper, actor and he wrote his own poetry.

   Analysis: Noun forms should be parallel.

   Action: Make the sentence parallel by eliminating the unnecessary verb at the end.

   Correction: The sentence should read:

   Tupac Shakur was a rapper, actor and poet.

4. The judge not only sentenced the prisoner to life he also confiscated his property.

   Analysis: Conjunctions like not only should be followed by "but also".

   Action: Make the sentence parallel by adding "but also".

   Correction: The sentence should read:

   The judge not only sentenced the prisoner to life but also confiscated his property.

5. Regardless of where they register or where they lived, voters must perform jury duty.

   Analysis: Confusion sometimes arises when past tense is inadvertently paired up with present tense.

   Action: Make the tenses agree.

   Correction: The sentence should read:

   Regardless of where they register or where they live, voters must perform jury duty.

6. Corporate shareholders seem more concerned with short-term profits than they do with long-term gains.

   Analysis: Some of the more difficult parallel structure questions stress finesse and simplicity.

   Action: Make the sentence simpler but eliminating the unnecessary "than they do with".

   Correction: The sentence should read:

   Corporate shareholders seem more concerned with short-term profits than long-term gains.

7. The main reasons criminals give for ending up in jail are that they had difficult childhoods in addition to leaving school at an early age.

   Analysis: Some of the more difficult parallel structure questions violate the shortest point rule and actually make the sentence longer — but tighter.

   Action: Make the sentence longer — but more parallel — by repeating the verb phrase "and that they".

   Correction: The sentence should read:

   The main reasons criminals give for ending up in jail are that they had difficult childhoods and that they had to leave school at an early age.

8. Jane went to the store to buy coffee, tea, in addition to milk.

   Analysis: Be careful when enumerating lists to stay parallel.

   Action: Eliminate the unnecessary "in addition to".

   Correction: The sentence should read:

   Jane went to the store to buy coffee, tea and milk.

9. Jane went to the store to buy coffee, tea, as well as milk.

   Analysis: Be careful when enumerating lists to stay parallel.

   Action: Eliminate the unnecessary "as well as".

   Correction: The sentence should read:

   Jane went to the store to buy coffee, tea and milk.

Mistaken Identity

Read, analyze and correct.

1. The novels of Ernest Hemingway are shorter than William Gaddis.

   Analysis: Is the comparison appropriate here?

   Action: Compare novels to novels, not novels to people.

   Correction: The sentence should read:

   The novels of Ernest Hemingway are shorter than the novels of William Gaddis.

   Or:

   The novels of Ernest Hemingway are shorter than those of William Gaddis.

2. *The Wire* is an infinitely more sophisticated TV series than *Keeping up with the Kardashians*.

   Analysis: Is the comparison appropriate here? Are we comparing one TV show to another?

   Action: None necessary.

Correction: The sentence is correct as is.

3. Breaking a leg requires more attention from a doctor than an arm.

   Analysis: Is the comparison appropriate here?

   Action: You can't compare an action (breaking) to an appendage (arm).

   Correction: The sentence should read:

   Breaking a leg requires more attention from a doctor than breaking an arm.

4. The skyscrapers in New York are bigger than San Francisco.

   Analysis: Is the comparison appropriate here?

   Action: You can't compare skyscrapers to cities.

   Correction: The sentence should read:

   The skyscrapers in New York are bigger than the skyscrapers in San Francisco.

   Or:

   The skyscrapers in New York are bigger than those in San Francisco.

5. Buying soda in six packs is usually cheaper than single bottles.

   Analysis: Is the comparison appropriate here?

   Action: You can't compare verbs (buying) to nouns (bottles).

   Correction: The sentence should read:

   Buying soda in six packs is usually cheaper than buying single bottles.

6. The duties of a soldier are more dangerous than a fire fighter.

   Analysis: Is the comparison appropriate here?

   Action: You can't compare duties to people.

   Correction: The sentence should read:

   The duties of a soldier are more dangerous than the duties of a fire fighter.

   Or:

   The duties of a soldier are more dangerous than those of a fire fighter.

≡

Who 'Dat

Read, analyze and correct.

1. When Franny and Zooey went for a winter walk, she forgot to bring her umbrella.

   Analysis: Who forgot her umbrella?

   Action: It's unclear whether the pronoun (she) refers to Franny or Zooey. Be specific.

   Correction: The sentence should read:

   When Franny and Zooey went for a winter walk, Franny forgot to bring her umbrella.

2. In New York City, they like bagels

   Analysis: Who likes bagels?

   Action: Be specific; use picture words.

   Correction: The sentence should read:

   In New York City, NYPD, construction workers and off-broadway actors like bagels.

3. It was so expensive that no one considered it reasonably priced.

   Analysis: What was so expensive?

   Action: There are too many vague and unnecessary its? Remember: It's not it!

   Correction: The sentence should read:

   The Vuitton bag was so expensive that no one considered the price reasonable.

4. Confiding in her close friend Marie, Jane found it annoying that she seemed to lose focus during the conversation.

   Analysis: Who lost focus, Jane or Marie?

   Action: Clarify the sentence structure.

   Correction: The sentence should read:

   Confiding in her close friend Marie, Jane found it annoying that Marie seemed to lose focus during the conversation.

5. The study of agricultural economics in college demands travel and fieldwork to foreign countries where they put academic theory into practice.

   Analysis: Who is putting theory into practice?

   Action: Be specific.

   Correction: The sentence should read:

   The study of agricultural economics in college demands travel and fieldwork to foreign countries where students put academic theory into practice.

6. John and James were walking to a restaurant, when, feeling sick, he decided to return home.

    Analysis: Who decided to return home, John or James?

    Action: Be specific.

    Correction: The sentence should read:

    John and James were walking to a restaurant, when, feeling sick, John decided to return home.

7. After Eminem released his "Relapse" album, he soon went back into the studio to record "Recovery".

    Analysis: Well, it's pretty clear who the rapper is, right? No problem.

    Action: None needed. There's no confusion here about who he refers to.

    Correction: OK as is.

8. By the time he finished dancing it in 1913, the Parisian audience was in an uproar.

    Analysis: Who finished dancing it in 1913. Eliminate the vague pronouns he and it.

    Action: Be specific; add details.

    Correction: The sentence should read:

    By the time Nijinsky finished dancing the "Rite of Spring" ballet in 1913, the Parisian audience was in an uproar.

Me Me Me

Read, analyze and correct.

1. The conversation was private, strictly between you and I.

    Analysis: Can't use subject pronouns after prepositions like between.

    Action: Use object pronouns instead.

    Correction: The sentence should read:

    The conversation was private, strictly between you and me.

2. The proclamation was addressed to you and we before anyone understood its contents.

    Analysis: Can't use subject pronouns after prepositions like to.

    Action: Use object pronouns instead.

    Correction: The sentence should read:

    The proclamation was addressed to you and us before anyone understood its contents.

3. The gourmet chef prepared a fancy vegetarian dinner for he and I.

   Analysis: Can't use subject pronouns after prepositions like for.

   Action: Use object pronouns instead.

   Correction: The sentence should read:

   The gourmet chef prepared a fancy vegetarian dinner for him and me.

4. Just between us, I think climate change is an inevitable process.

   Analysis: Must use object pronouns after prepositions like between.

   Action: None required.

   Correction: OK as is.

5. Delivering the message to you and she was an act of bravery.

   Analysis: Can't use subject pronouns after prepositions like to.

   Action: Use object pronouns instead.

   Correction: The sentence should read:

   Delivering the message to you and her was an act of bravery.

Joined at the Hip

Read, analyze and correct. Recall that Comma Splice refers to two sentences incorrectly connected by a comma. Use a semicolon to make part of one sentence subordinate to the other.

1. San Francisco is a small city with a large population, this results in a great deal of traffic congestion.

   Analysis: Can't have two sentences separated with a comma. Think semicolon or subordination.

   Action: Two options: Use a semicolon OR use subordination.

   Correction: The sentence should read:

   San Francisco is a small city with a large population; this results in a great deal of traffic congestion.

   Or:

   San Francisco is a small city with a large population, resulting in a great deal of traffic congestion.

2. Crossing into the jungles of Venezuela, explorers encountered numerous indigenous people, the most ferocious were the Yanomami.

   Analysis: Can't have two sentences separated with a comma.

   Action: Think semicolon.

   Correction: The sentence should read:

   Crossing into the jungles of Venezuela, explorers encountered numerous indigenous people; the most ferocious were the Yanomami.

3. Star athletes from many countries competed for a spot on the Olympic team, the goal of each was to receive a gold medal.

   Analysis: Can't have two sentences separated with a comma.

   Action: Subordinate one sentence to the other.

   Correction: The sentence should read:

   Star athletes from many countries competed for a spot on the Olympic team, each hoping to receive a gold medal.

4. Many people think that Woodrow Wilson proclaimed that World War I was the "War to end all wars." — in fact, it was H.G. Wells.

   Analysis: Can't have two sentences separated with a comma.

   Action: Think semicolon.

   Correction: The sentence should read:

   Many people think that Woodrow Wilson proclaimed that World War I was the "War to end all wars"; in fact, it was H.G. Wells.

5. Traveling to Egypt, archeologists discovered many ancient treasures, they are housed in museums around the world.

   Analysis: Can't have two sentences separated with a comma.

   Action: Subordinate one sentence to the other.

   Correction: The sentence should read:

   Traveling to Egypt, archeologists discovered many ancient treasures, which are now housed in museums around the world.

6. Uccello was one of the greatest painters of the Fifteenth century; his works are on display in museums throughout Europe.

   Analysis: Nice use of the semicolon!

   Action: None required.

   Correction: OK as is. BTW, if you ever get to Florence, be sure to see *The Battle of San Remo* in the Uffizi museum. Stunning.

4—Cheat Sheet

By this time, you should be feeling pretty good about the 9 main grammar rules. You might want to just stand back for a moment, take stock in what you've learned and contemplate the Big Picture. So here are the rules once again, this time presented in a nutshell with titles in short-hand form.

Leaking Oil

Concept: The first noun after the comma must refer back to the action described.

- **wrong** — Leaking oil, the mechanic fixed the car.
- **correct** — Leaking oil, the car was fixed by the mechanic.

Matching Pairs

Concept: Singular subjects need singular verbs; plural subjects need plural verbs
Corollary: Delete prepositional phrases between the subject and verb.

- **wrong** -- The harmful effects of saturated fat on the arterial system is well known.
- **correct** — The harmful effects of saturated fat on the arterial system are well known.

Avoid Alien Beings

Concept: For SAT grammar, never use "being" if you can help it.

- **wrong** — Until being nominated for an award, the actor was a virtual unknown.
- **correct** — Until he was nominated for an award, the actor was a virtual unknown.

Shortest Point

Concept: For SAT English, shorter is almost always better.
Exception: Parallel structure sometimes requires more words for consistency.

≡

- **awkward** — Kate had finished washing the dishes and then she took out the trash.
- **correct** — When Kate finished washing the dishes, she took out the trash.

Apples and Oranges

Concept — Keep nouns in parallel or verbs in parallel; don't mix the two.

- **wrong** — Mary studies history, literature and likes to paint
- **correct** — Mary studies history, literature and painting

Mistaken Identity

Concept — Compare like nouns.

- **wrong** — The weather in California is better than Canada
- **correct** — The weather in California is better than the weather in Canada

Who 'Dat

Concept — Get directly to the point; avoid unnecessary or vague pronouns.
Corollary — Watch out for unnecessary "its" littering the grammar landscape. It's not it!

- **wrong** -- When she fell down the rabbit hole, she entered a world of illusion
- **correct** -- When Alice fell down the rabbit hole, she entered a world of illusion

Me Me Me

Concept — Subjects and subject pronouns never follow prepositions.

- **wrong** — for you and I, between you and he, with you and she, about you and they, etc. etc.
- **correct** — for you and ME, between you and him, with you and her, about you and them

Joined at the Hip

Concept — No comma between two separate sentences. Comma splice.

- **wrong** — San Francisco is a small city with a large population, this results in a great deal of traffic congestion.
- **correct** — San Francisco is a small city with a large population, resulting in a great deal of traffic congestion.

5—Jumbles

Are you ready to jumble! So far we've been working in the shallow end of the pool. You've learned the 9 main grammar rules and had a chance to practice them in context. You've even see the rules condensed to two pages in the Cheat Sheet chapter.

Now we take off the water wings and dive into the deep end. In these jumbles, you'll see previous questions from all the different grammar rules mixed together. Your job is to stay afloat and select the correct answer.

Note: As on the SAT grammar test, the first selection below simply repeats the question.

Jumble 1

1. The novels of Ernest Hemingway are shorter than William Gaddis.

    (a) The novels of Ernest Hemingway are shorter than William Gaddis.
    (b) The novels of Ernest Hemingway which are shorter than William Gaddis.
    (c) The novels of Ernest Hemingway are shorter than those of William Gaddis.
    (d) The novels of Ernest Hemingway being shorter than William Gaddis is.

2. When Franny and Zooey went for a winter walk, she forgot to bring her umbrella.

    (a) When Franny and Zooey went for a winter walk, she forgot to bring her umbrella.
    (b) When Franny and Zooey went for a winter walk, it was she that forgot to bring her umbrella.
    (c) When Franny and Zooey went for a winter walk, the umbrella had been forgotten by her.
    (d) When Franny and Zooey went for a winter walk, Franny forgot to bring her umbrella.

49

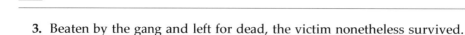

3. Beaten by the gang and left for dead, the victim nonetheless survived.

   (a) Beaten by the gang and left for dead, the victim nonetheless survived.
   (b) Beaten by the gang and being left for dead, the victim nonetheless survived.
   (c) Left for dead after being beaten by the gang, the victim nonetheless survived.
   (d) After she being beaten by the gang and she was left for dead, the victim nonetheless survived.

4. As a boy, my grandma read me bedtime stories.

   (a) As a boy, my grandma read me bedtime stories.
   (b) As a boy, bedtime stories were read to me by my grandma.
   (c) As a boy, I was read bedtime stories by my grandma.
   (d) As a boy, my grandma read bedtime stories to me.

5. Each of the dogs bound in leather harnesses were ready to depart.

   (a) Each of the dogs bound in leather harnesses were ready to depart.
   (b) Each of the dogs bound in it's leather harness were ready to depart.
   (c) Each of the dogs bound in leather harnesses was ready to depart.
   (d) Each of the dogs bound in leather harnesses in it's cages were ready to depart.

6. The athlete being strong was better than being fast.

   (a) The athlete being strong was better than being fast.
   (b) The athlete thought strength was better than being fast.
   (c) The athlete thought strength was better than speed.
   (d) The athlete thought strong was a better thing than speed.

7. The conversation was private, strictly between you and I.

   (a) The conversation was private, strictly between you and I.
   (b) The conversation was private, strictly between you and me.
   (c) The conversation was strictly between you and me, privately.
   (d) The private conversation was private, strictly between you and me.

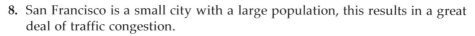

8. San Francisco is a small city with a large population, this results in a great deal of traffic congestion.

   (a) San Francisco is a small city with a large population, this results in a great deal of traffic congestion.
   (b) San Francisco is a small city with a large population, as a consequence there's a great deal of traffic congestion.
   (c) San Francisco is a small city with a large population, resulting in a great deal of traffic congestion.
   (d) San Francisco is a small city with a large population, it has a great deal of traffic congestion.

Answers

The correct answers for Jumble 1 are given below along with the grammar rule the question exemplifies.

1. Answer: C

    The novels of Ernest Hemingway are shorter than those of William Gaddis (rule: mistaken identity — parallel structure)

2. Answer: D

    When Franny and Zooey went for a winter walk, Franny forgot to bring her umbrella (rule: who 'dat — indefinite pronouns).

3. Answer: A (no error)

    Beaten by the gang and left for dead, the victim nonetheless survived. (rule: avoid alien beings — use active verbs)

4. Answer: C

    As a boy, I was read bedtime stories by my grandma (rule: leaking oil — misplaced modifiers).

5. Answer: C

    Each of the dogs bound in leather harnesses was ready to depart. (rule: subject verb agreement — matching pairs).

6. Answer: C

    The athlete thought strength was better than speed. (rule: avoid alien beings — use active verbs).

7. Answer: B

    The conversation was private, strictly between you and me. (rule: me me me — subject pronouns never follow prepositions)

8. Answer: C

    San Francisco is a small city with a large population, resulting in a great deal of traffic congestion. (rule: joined at the hip — comma splice).

Jumble 2

1. The effects of sugar on insulin resistance is observed in many diabetics.

    (a) The effects of sugar on insulin resistance is observed in many diabetics.
    (b) The effects of sugar on insulin resistance are observed in many diabetics.
    (c) The effects of sugar on insulin resistance is observing in many diabetics.
    (d) The effects of sugar on insulin resistance has been observed in many diabetics.

2. The captain of the ship, being asleep at the wheel, failed in his maritime duties.

    (a) The captain of the ship, being asleep at the wheel, failed in his maritime duties.
    (b) Being asleep at the wheel, the ship's captain failed in its maritime duties.
    (c) Asleep at the wheel, the captain of the ship failed in his maritime duties.
    (d) Being the captain of the ship, asleep at the wheel, he failed in his maritime duties.

3. The best way to get an exact answer to the question would be to use a calculator.

    (a) The best way to get an exact answer to the question would be to use a calculator.
    (b) The best way to get an exact answer to the question would be in the use of a calculator.
    (c) The use of a calculator being the best way to get an exact answer to the question.
    (d) Using a calculator is the best way to get an exact answer.

4. Breaking a leg requires more attention from a doctor than a finger.

    (a) Breaking a leg requires more attention from a doctor than a finger.
    (b) Breaking a leg requires a doctor to pay more attention to you than he does to a finger.
    (c) Breaking a leg requires a doctor to pay more attention to it than a finger.
    (d) Breaking a leg requires more attention from a doctor than breaking a finger.

5. In New York, they like bagels.

    (a) In New York, they like bagels.
    (b) In New York, construction workers like bagels.
    (c) In New York, bagels are it.
    (d) In New York, bagels are what some people like to eat.

6. Throwing a temper tantrum, the teacher reprimanded the four-year-old.

   (a) Throwing a temper tantrum, the teacher reprimanded the four-year-old.
   (b) Throwing a temper tantrum, the teacher was reprimanded by the four-year-old.
   (c) Throwing a temper tantrum, the teacher she reprimanded the four-year-old.
   (d) Throwing a temper tantrum, the four-year-old was reprimanded by the teacher.

7. The first of many issues debated by the House of Representatives is on CNN today.

   (a) The first of many issues debated by the House of Representatives is on CNN today.
   (b) The first of many issues debated by the House of Representatives are on CNN today.
   (c) The first of many issues which are to be debated by the House of Representatives are on CNN today.
   (d) The first of many issues debated by the House of Representatives are on CNN today.

8. The proclamation was addressed to you and we before anyone understood its contents.

   (a) The proclamation was addressed to you and we before anyone understood its contents.
   (b) The proclamation was addressed to you and us before anyone understood its contents.
   (c) The proclamation was addressed to you and she before anyone understood its contents.
   (d) The proclamation was addressed to you and they before anyone understood its contents.

9. Crossing into Venezuela, explorers encountered indigenous people, the most ferocious were the Yanomami.

   (a) Crossing into Venezuela, explorers encountered a variety of indigenous people, the most ferocious were the Yanomami.
   (b) Crossing into Venezuela, a variety of indigenous people were encountered, the most ferocious were the Yanomami
   (c) Crossing into Venezuela, explorers encountered a variety of indigenous people, the most ferocious were the Yanomami.
   (d) Crossing into Venezuela, explorers encountered a variety of indigenous people; the most ferocious were the Yanomami.

Answers

The correct answers for Jumble 2 are given below along with the grammar rule the question exemplifies.

1. Answer: B

   The effects of sugar on insulin resistance are observed in many diabetics. (rule: subject verb agreement — matching pairs)

2. Answer: C

   Asleep at the wheel, the captain of the ship failed in his maritime duties. (rule: avoid alien beings — use active words)

3. Answer: D

   Using a calculator is the best way to get an exact answer. (rule: shortest point — economy of expression).

4. Answer: D

   Breaking a leg requires more attention from a doctor than breaking a finger. (rule: apples and oranges — parallel structure)

5. Answer: B.

   In New York, construction workers like bagels. (rule: who 'dat — indefinite pronouns)

6. Answer: D

   Throwing a temper tantrum, the four-year-old was reprimanded by the teacher. (rule: leaking oil — misplaced modifiers)

7. Answer: A(no error)

   The first of many issues debated by the House of Representatives is on CNN today. (rule: subject verb agreement — matching pairs)

8. Answer: B

   The proclamation was addressed to you and us before anyone understood its contents. (rule: me me me — subject pronouns never follow prepositions)

9. Answer: D

   Crossing into Venezuela, explorers encountered a variety of indigenous people; the most ferocious were the Yanomami. (rule:joined at the hip — comma splice)

6—Practice Test

By now, having circled through the grammar rules in several different ways, you're ready to apply the concepts and techniques you've learned in a simulated SAT environment. The following SAT-style practice test was specifically designed to reinforce the rules and analysis presented in this book.

The practice test comprises three parts: Improving Sentences, Finding the Mistake, Improving Paragraphs. Select the correct answer in each section.

Improving Sentences

Directions: The following sentences test correctness and effectiveness of expression. For each question in this section, select the best answer from among the choices given.

1. Many of the world's greatest paintings, such as Boticelli's Venus and Uccello's Battle of San Remo, <u>are in the process of being displayed at the Uffizi gallery in Florence</u>.

   (a) are in the process of being displayed at the Uffizi gallery in Florence
   (b) should be displayed at the Uffizi gallery in Florence
   (c) are on display at the Uffizi gallery in Florence
   (d) are being displayed at the Uffizi gallery in Florence
   (e) have been displaying at the Uffizi gallery in Florence

2. Returning home from a long vacation, <u>the bags were unceremoniously dropped in the hallway by weary family members</u>.

    (a) the bags were unceremoniously dropped in the hallway by weary family members
    (b) the bag was dropped unceremoniously in the hallway by weary family members
    (c) weary family members unceremoniously dropped their bags in the hallway
    (d) the bags they were unceremoniously dropped in the hallway by weary family members
    (e) weary family members unceremoniously dropping bags in the hallway

3. <u>Low levels of leptin in the blood stream helps control</u> the onset of obesity and similar metabolic disorders.

    (a) Low levels of leptin in the blood stream helps controls
    (b) Low levels of leptin in the blood stream help control
    (c) Low levels of leptin helps in the blood stream controlling
    (d) Low levels of leptin in the blood stream helping control
    (e) Low levels of leptin in the blood stream helps in controlling

4. <u>Fast on the draw, Billy the Kid was a famous outlaw of the old west, only Jesse James, the leader of a gang famous for robbing trains, had more notoriety.</u>

    (a) Fast on the draw, Billy the Kid was a famous outlaw of the old west, only Jesse James, the leader of a gang famous for robbing trains, had more notoriety.
    (b) Fast on the draw, Billy the Kid was a famous outlaw of the old west and only Jesse James, the leader of a gang famous for robbing trains, could have had more notoriety.
    (c) Fast on the draw, Billy the Kid was a famous outlaw of the old west, but Jesse James was the leader of a gang famous for robbing trains and had more notoriety.
    (d) Fast on the draw, Billy the Kid was a famous outlaw of the old west; only Jesse James, the leader of a gang famous for robbing trains, had more notoriety.
    (e) Fast on the draw, Billy the Kid was as famous an outlaw of the old west as was Jesse James, only he was the leader of a gang famous for robbing trains and had more notoriety.

5. <u>Information from police ledgers and databases suggest criminal behavior increases under the influence of the full moon</u>.

   (a) Information from police ledgers and databases suggest criminal behavior increases under the influence of the full moon.
   (b) Informations from police ledgers and databases suggest criminal behavior increases under the influence of the full moon.
   (c) Information from police ledgers and databases suggests criminal behavior increases under the influence of the full moon.
   (d) Information from police ledgers and databases is suggesting criminal behavior increases under the influence of the full moon.
   (e) Information from police ledgers and databases has suggested criminal behavior under the influence of the full moon.

6. Cornelius Vanderbilt, who established public libraries across the nation, <u>was not only a ruthless industrialist but he was a well-known philanthropist</u>.

   (a) was not only a ruthless industrialist but he was a well-known philanthropist
   (b) was not only a ruthless industrialist but also a well-known philanthropist
   (c) was not only a ruthless industrialist but well-known as a philanthropist
   (d) was not only a ruthless industrialist but he is also a well-known philanthropist
   (e) was only a ruthless industrialist but also a well-known philanthropist

7. As requested, the pastry chef <u>cooked a souffle for you and I that was out of this world</u>.

   (a) cooked a souffle for you and I that was out of this world
   (b) cooked you and I a souffle that was out of this world
   (c) cooked a souffle for you and me that was out of this world
   (d) cooked a souffle for us and I thought that it was out of this world
   (e) cooked a souffle for you and I that was out of this world

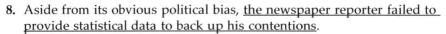

8. Aside from its obvious political bias, <u>the newspaper reporter failed to provide statistical data to back up his contentions</u>.

   (a) the newspaper reporter failed to provide statistical data to back up his contentions
   (b) the newspaper reporter had been failed to provide statistical data to back up his contentions
   (c) the newspaper failed to provide statistical data to back up his contentions
   (d) the newspaper failed to provide statistical data to back up its contentions
   (e) the newspaper failed to provide statistics and data that would back up the reporter's contentions

9. Retail establishments attempt to influence consumer purchases <u>not only by product placement but also giving store discounts</u>.

   (a) not only by product placement but also giving store discounts
   (b) not only by product placement but also they give store discounts
   (c) not only by product placement but also by giving store discounts
   (d) not by product placement but only by giving store discounts
   (e) not only by product placement but giving store discounts as well

10. Movie producers seem more concerned with <u>the box office returns of a film rather than how artistic it is</u>.

    (a) the box office returns of a film rather than how artistic it is
    (b) the box office returns of a film rather whether it is artistic
    (c) the box office returns of how well an artistic film is
    (d) the box office returns of a film rather than how artistic it is
    (e) the box office returns of a film rather than its artistic value

11. After the banker notified the student that his loan request had been denied, <u>he suggested that the form be resubmitted with a co-signer</u>.

    (a) he suggested that the form be resubmitted with a co-signer
    (b) the banker suggested it be resubmitted by him with a co-signer
    (c) the student suggested that the banker resubmit it with a co-signer
    (d) the form was suggested to be resubmitted with a co-signer
    (e) the banker suggested that the student resubmit the form with a co-signer

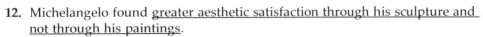

12. Michelangelo found <u>greater aesthetic satisfaction through his sculpture and not through his paintings</u>.

   (a) greater aesthetic satisfaction through his sculpture and not through his paintings
   (b) his sculpture had greater aesthetic satisfaction and not his paintings
   (c) his paintings were of greater aesthetic satisfaction than through his paintings
   (d) greater aesthetic satisfaction through his sculpture than through his paintings
   (e) greater aesthetic satisfaction throughout his sculpture than throughout his paintings

Finding the Mistake

Directions: The following sentences test your ability to recognize grammar and usage errors. Each sentence contains either a single error or no error at all.

1. <u>A team of</u> scientists working <u>feverishly</u> at the CERN research center <u>in</u>
   ❶   **❷**   **❸**
   Switzerland <u>have</u> recently discovered evidence of the elusive Higgs Boson.
                ❹

   <u>No error.</u>
   ❺

2. <u>Regardless of</u> where they went to school or <u>what</u> their final occupation <u>is,</u>
   ❶   **❷**   **❸**
   today's college graduates are <u>saddled with</u> enormous debt.
                                  ❹

   <u>No error.</u>
   ❺

3. Politicians <u>who</u> vote along party lines <u>do it</u> because <u>they</u> don't
               ❶   **❷**   **❸**
   want to be seen <u>as pariahs.</u>   <u>No error.</u>
                    ❹   **❺**

61

4. <u>When</u> job opportunities dwindle and unemployment <u>among</u> middle class
   ❶   **❷**

   workers <u>increase</u>, the government <u>has</u> a responsibility to provide short-
             ❸   **❹**

   term relief.   <u>No error.</u>
                         ❺

5. Henry James, an <u>accomplished</u> novelist and brother <u>to</u> William James,
                      ❶   **❷**

   wrote <u>nuanced</u> stories about the culture and behavior of <u>upper crust</u> society.
           ❸   **❹**

   figures.   <u>No error.</u>
                     ❺

6. Just across the river <u>was</u> the campgrounds of the soldiers, many <u>of whom</u>
                           ❶   **❷**

   now rested in <u>their</u> tents, exhausted by weeks of <u>deadly</u> combat.
                   ❸   **❹**

   <u>No error.</u>
     ❺

7. <u>Between</u> lions and tigers, tigers <u>are</u> the <u>strongest</u>, lions are the <u>weaker</u>.
     ❶   **❷**   **❸**   **❹**
   <u>No error.</u>
     ❺

8. Many scientists now <u>agree</u> that carbon emissions <u>alone</u> are not the only
                         ❶   **❷**

   functions which <u>was</u> responsible for the <u>rise of</u> global warming.
                     ❸   **❹**

   <u>No error.</u>
     ❺

9. Albert Schweitzer, a <u>recipient</u> of the Nobel Prize in 1952, was
                          ❶

   <u>a philosopher</u>, <u>missionary</u> and he <u>practiced medicine</u> in Africa.
     ❷   **❸**   **❹**
   <u>No error.</u>
     ❺

10. When Marx wrote the communist <u>manifesto,</u> his detractors criticized the
    ❶
    premise <u>being</u> that workers <u>had</u> nothing to lose but <u>their</u> chains.
    ❷   **❸**   **❹**
    <u>No error.</u>
    ❺

11. More often <u>than not,</u> <u>it's</u> faster to take a plane than <u>driving</u> a car <u>long</u>
    ❶   **❷**   **❸**   **❹**
    distances.   <u>No error.</u>
                      ❺

12. With you <u>and me</u> in attendance, the ceremony, after <u>some delay,</u> <u>took</u>
    ❶   **❷**   **❸**
    place <u>in</u> the outdoor garden.   <u>No error.</u>
    ❹   **❺**

13. <u>Written by</u> Homer after the fall of Troy, the "Odyessy" describes the
    ❶
    <u>plight</u> of <u>greek</u> sailors and their leader Odysseus attempting to find <u>his</u>
    ❷   **❸**   **❹**
    way home.   <u>No error.</u>
                     ❺

14. The <u>volume of</u> bad loans made to <u>unsecured</u> creditors in the housing
    ❶   **❷**
    market <u>emphasize</u> the need for more stringent <u>federal</u> regulations.
           ❸   **❹**
    <u>No error.</u>
    ❺

15. Physicists today, <u>unlike 20 years ago,</u> give <u>credence</u> to string theory, a
    ❶   **❷**
    concept <u>once</u> held in ridicule for <u>its</u> practical and experimental limitations.
    ❸   **❹**
    <u>No error.</u>
    ❺

63

16. <u>When</u> running for office, <u>voters</u> choose members of congress <u>who</u> seem to
    ❶   **❷**   **❸**
    have their <u>constituents'</u> best interests at heart.
                 ❹

    <u>No error.</u>
        ❺

17. Australopithecus, which <u>evolved in</u> eastern Africa, emerged some 2.3
                              ❶

    million <u>years</u> ago and <u>apparently</u> gave rise to <u>we</u> humans beings.
            ❷   **❸**   **❹**

    <u>No error.</u>
        ❺

18. In Death Valley, <u>one</u> of the <u>hotter</u> areas in the United States, food and
                     ❶   **❷**

    water are in <u>such</u> short supply that <u>both</u> man and animals must struggle to
                 ❸   **❹**

    survive.   <u>No error.</u>
                                     ❺

Improving Paragraphs

Directions: The following passage is an early draft of an essay. Read the passage and select the best answers for the questions that follow.

❶ Nutrition is in a state of flux today. ❷ Many claims made by experts that were prevailing during the previous decade have come under attack. ❸ Complex carbohydrates, once the darling of mainstream nutritionists, are now the subject of heated debate.

❹ It is pointed out by some that grains, particularly wheat, cause children to have allergic reactions. ❺ Apparently new, genetically modified strains of so-called dwarf wheat is playing havoc with our immune system. ❻ This supposedly gives rise to celiac disease and other metabolic disorders.

❼ If that weren't bad enough, fats, once the scourge of dieters everywhere, have now gained new appreciation. ❽ According to some researchers, fat may not make you fat. ❾ Scientists now point to a complex feedback loop in fat metabolism whereby leptin, an appetite suppressant, is released by fat cells. ❿ Many researchers have reported these findings, they say the results represent a major breakthrough in understanding appetite control.

⓫ What are we to think of these findings? ⓬ If complex carbohydrates are bad for you and I and fats are actually beneficial, does that mean we should all douse our steaks with cream sauce and load up on lobster? ⓭ Not yet, at least according to heart specialists, who still worry about clogged arteries in the general population. ⓮ It's a daunting task for people to try to make sense of all this conflicting information.

1. What should be done with sentence 2 (reproduced below)?
   Many claims made by experts that were prevailing during the previous decade have come under attack.

   (a) Insert "these days" after "attack."
   (b) Insert "of this sort" after Many claims"
   (c) Change "during the previous decade" to "in the previous decade."
   (d) Delete "that were prevailing."
   (e) No change.

2. Which is the best way to deal with sentence 4 (reproduced below)?
It is pointed out by some that grains, particularly wheat, cause children to have allergic reactions.

   (a) Leave it as is.
   (b) Change "It is pointed out by some" to "Scientists point out."
   (c) Add "for scientists" to the end of the sentence.
   (d) Delete the sentence.
   (e) Change "particularly wheat" to "wheat, in particular."

3. What is the best way to revise the underlined portion of sentence 5 (reproduced below)?
Apparently new, genetically modified strains of so-called dwarf wheat is playing havoc with our immune systems.

   (a) Delete "so-called."
   (b) Change "playing havoc with" to "destroying the functional capabilities of."
   (c) Change "is playing" to "are playing."
   (d) Change "dwarf wheat" to "vertically challenged wheat."
   (e) No change.

4. In context, which of the following is the best way to revise sentence 10 (reproduced below)?
Many researchers have reported these findings, they say the results represent a major breakthrough in understanding appetite control.

   (a) Leave it as is.
   (b) Reporting these findings on appetite control, researchers have said, is a major breakthrough in understand it.
   (c) Understanding these findings, say many researchers, represent a major breakthrough in understanding.
   (d) It's a major breakthrough for many reporters who say that understanding appetite control is their finding.
   (e) Many researchers have reported these findings; they say the results represent a major breakthrough in understanding appetite control.

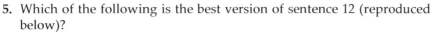

5. Which of the following is the best version of sentence 12 (reproduced below)?

   If complex carbohydrates are bad for you and I and fats are actually beneficial, does that mean we should all douse our steaks with cream sauce and load up on lobster.

   (a) Leave it as is.
   (b) Change "does that mean" to "doesn't it make more sense that."
   (c) Change "for you and I" to "for you and me."
   (d) Delete the sentence.
   (e) Change "complex carbohydrates" to "potatoes, sweet potatoes, white rice, brown rice, wild rice, yams and other forms of starch."

6. Which of the following would make the most logical conclusion to this essay.

   It's a daunting task for people to make sense of all this conflicting information.

   (a) It's hard for most people to make sense of all this often conflicting information.
   (b) Most people need to think long and hard about this information, often conflicting.
   (c) For individuals like myself, who find it daunting, it's difficult to make sense of all this.
   (d) Making sense of this apparently conflicting information is a daunting task.
   (e) Conflicting information makes this task daunting for people trying to make sense of it.

≡

Answers

Correct answers to the practice test are provided below:

Improving Sentences

1. **(c)** Many of the world's greatest paintings, such as Botticelli's Venus and Uccello's Battle of San Remo, are on display at the Uffizi gallery in Florence.

2. **(c)** Returning home from a long vacation, weary family members unceremoniously dropped their bags in the hallway.

3. **(b)** Low levels of leptin in the blood stream help control the onset of obesity and similar metabolic disorders.

4. **(d)** Fast on the draw, Billy the Kid was a famous outlaw of the old west; only Jesse James, the leader of a gang famous for robbing trains, had more notoriety.

5. **(c)** Information from police ledgers and databases suggests criminal behavior increases under the influence of the full moon.

6. **(b)** Cornelius Vanderbilt, who established public libraries across the nation, was not only a ruthless industrialist but also a well-known philanthropist.

7. **(c)** As requested, the pastry chef cooked a souffle for you and him that was out of this world.

8. **(d)** Aside from its obvious political bias, the newspaper failed to provide statistical data to back up its contentions.

9. **(e)** In China the responsibilities of national politicians are more numerous than those of local party members.

10. **(e)** Movie producers seem more concerned with the box office returns of a film rather than with its artistic value.

11. **(c)** After authorizing funds for a college loan, the lending officer was thanked by the student, now ready for college.

12. **(d)** Michelangelo found greater aesthetic satisfaction through his sculpture than through his paintings.

Finding the Mistake

1. **(④)** A team of scientists working feverishly at the CERN research center in Switzerland has recently discovered evidence of the elusive Higgs Boson.

2. **(③)** Regardless of where they went to school or what their final occupation was, today's college graduates are saddled with enormous debt.

3. (**2**) Politicians who vote along party lines do so because they don't want to be seen as pariahs.

4. (**3**) When job opportunities dwindle and unemployment among middle class workers increases, the government has a responsibility to provide short-term relief.

5. (**5**) Henry James, an accomplished novelist and brother to William James, wrote nuanced stories about the culture and behavior of upper crust society figures.

6. (**2**) Just across the river were the campgrounds of the soldiers, many of whom now rested in their tents, exhausted by weeks of deadly combat.

7. (**3**) Between lions and tigers, tigers are the stronger, lions are the weaker.

8. (**5**) Because she was worried about appearing before the committee, Hillary was absent from the initial sessions held on capital hill.

9. (**4**) Albert Schweitzer, a recipient of the Nobel Prize in 1952, was a philosopher, missionary and medical practitioner in Africa.

10. (**2**) When Marx wrote the communist manifesto, his detractors criticized the premise that workers had nothing to lose but their chains.

11. (**3**) More often than not, it's faster to take a plane than to drive a car long distances.

12. (**5**) After some delay, the ceremony took place in the outdoor garden with both Sally and me in attendance.

13. (**4**) Written by Homer after the fall of Troy, the "Odyssey" describes the plight of Greek sailors and their leader, Odysseus, attempting to find their way home.

14. (**3**) The volume of bad loans made to unsecured creditors in the housing market emphasizes the need for more stringent federal regulations.

15. (**1**) Physicists today, unlike those of 20 years ago, give credence to string theory, a concept once held in ridicule for its practical and experimental limitations.

16. (**2**) When running for office, members of congress who seem to have their constituents' best interests at heart are chosen by voters.

17. (**3**) Australopithecus, most experts agree, emerged from eastern Africa some 2.3 million years ago and apparently gave rise to us, the people now inhabiting the earth.

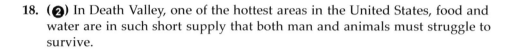

18. (**2**) In Death Valley, one of the hottest areas in the United States, food and water are in such short supply that both man and animals must struggle to survive.

Improving Paragraphs

1. (**4**) Many claims made by experts during the previous decade have come under attack.

2. (**2**) Scientists point out that grains, particularly wheat, cause children to have allergic reactions

3. (**3**) Apparently new, genetically modified strains of so-called dwarf wheat are playing havoc with our immune systems.

4. (**5**) Many researchers have reported these findings; they say the results represent a major breakthrough in understanding appetite control.

5. (**3**) If complex carbohydrates are bad for you and me and fats are actually beneficial, does that mean we should all douse our steaks with cream sauce and load up on lobster?

6. (**4**) Making sense of this apparently conflicting information is a daunting task.

21825307R00041

Made in the USA
San Bernardino, CA
07 June 2015